THE
NOVEL
IN
YOU

ALSO
BY
ROSALIND
BRACKENBURY

NOVELS
Becoming George Sand
The House in Morocco
Windstorm and Flood
Seas Outside the Reef
The Circus at the End of the World

SHORT STORIES
Between Man and Woman Keys

CHILDREN'S BOOKS
The True Story of Henrietta Penelope Hen

POETRY
The Dancing Party
The Beautiful Routes of the West
Yellow Swing

THE
NOVEL
IN
YOU

A novelist's guide to writing better fiction.

BY
Rosalind Brackenbury

ANTAEUS BOOKS

ISBN 978-0-9828591-8-6
Library of Congress Control Number: 2011906130

Illustrations by Miranda Brackenbury
Author photo by Carol Tedesco

Book design by Amy McAdams
www.amymcadams.com

www.AntaeusBooks.com
publisher@AntaeusBooks.com

*...for all the novelists who have given me such pleasure
in a life-time of reading.*

And for my students, at the Studios of Key West and elsewhere.

*A novelist…can be a mighty liar and
a mighty truth-teller, at the same time and
in the same sentence.*
JULIAN BARNES

First we read; then we write.
EMERSON

CONTENTS

INTRODUCTION

If you are reading this, you have probably written some fiction already; and you are probably a reader.

This book is for writers and readers. Really, that's just two aspects of the same person. To write, you must read. It's reading the work of others that feeds writers, inspires us and keeps us in touch with the time in which we live.

Writing a novel is easy, it's also hard, it's fun and it's also often despairing. It's one of the most exciting things you can do, and it's endless work. Incredible numbers of people want to do it, and few actually do. If you want to find the wannabees, just say you're a writer, at a party, to your neighbor on an airplane, to the next person in line at the grocery store. "Oh", I always wanted to be a writer! This is one frequent response. Another: "I have so many stories inside me!" A third, " Should I have heard of you?" which is really unanswerable. Few people go around saying out loud that they wish they were heart surgeons or bus drivers or tennis stars, but a good section of the population wishes they were writers. It seems that the urge to tell a story is universal; also the assumption is that if you have written a novel you must be both rich and famous.

I have to start by saying that the reverse is usually true, that you almost certainly will not get rich, and famous is these days reserved for movie stars, musicians, politicians and criminals.

But the next thing to say is that yes, writing a novel IS all it's cracked up to be, because nothing quite beats adding to the world's store of literature. No, there isn't too much already, and there never will be. As with painting, music, photography, dance, it is simply what humans want to do, tell stories to each other, amuse, inform, alarm and entertain; add another insight to the business of being human.

Reading

Many writers begin to write when young simply because they love reading, or being read to. We all learn from imitation, whether it's only how to get food into our mouths or how to put our clothes on. As writers we need to be reading, learning from reading. Read all the time, on the beach, in the back yard, on the toilet, in the bath, in bed. Read everything you can lay your hands on and enjoy. Don't bother with the books you don't enjoy: life is too short to force-feed yourself, and some books are just not worth it. Follow your own greed and passion for the stories and the writing that turn you on. Read as a professional. See what others are doing, and why. Learn from them: why is that a good beginning? Why did he/she end the book that way? How have you been made to feel about a certain character?

What is the narrator trying to do, and has it worked? Why did you want to put the book down halfway through? Why, on the other hand, could you hardly bear to put another down at all? We don't all love the same things (or the same people, luckily) and we don't have the same attitudes to life. Reading is discovering your own attitude, your own pleasure, your own questions, and perhaps answers. Read awarely, thoughtfully, and you will learn what makes a good, or a great novel, and why some of the blockbusters are not worth your attention. Don't worry about "catching" a certain writer's style. This will no doubt happen, we all spend time trying to sound like Hemingway, or Virginia Woolf, or Philip Roth or even Stephen King at various times of our lives; but this will pass. A lot gets said about "finding your voice" in writing workshops, but each of us already has a voice, the way we have a certain walk, or gestures, or accent. Reading, you can learn from the writers you admire, and move on. Because you will move on, into a surer and clearer version of yourself, until whoever reads you on the page will recognize your own, unique style.

(All the writers mentioned in this book may not be familiar to you: I suggest using Google and/or Wikipedia to find out who they are/were, and then ordering books from your local library. I have listed a few excellent books on writing and fiction at the end of the book; there are many more, but these are ones I've found particularly stimulating.)

1. BEGINNING

The first session, or chapter, has to be about Beginning. Now, the page or paragraph that will actually begin your finished novel will most likely not be the one you actually started out with. So, don't get too hung up on a good beginning. When you are beginning to write, just plunge in. Begin anywhere. What matters is simply to get going, to get the story started. Begin, and keep going. Later, much later, you can make the decision about whether this is where you actually want to Begin.

Keeping going is the main thing, once you have started. Imagine you have a car which you have jump-started, and it's running fine, but if you let the engine quit, it will take all that effort to start again.

Getting an Idea

But starting – how does that happen? My advice is, to go for a walk or a swim, lie in a bath, lie on some grass under a tree, take your attention off the whole thing. Exercise works really well, so does housework. Cut the grass, wash the car. Dream in a hammock. Watch the ocean. Go to an art gallery, or a movie. Then, one day, one moment, you will have an Idea. It will strike you, and at this point you can rush home or get dry or stop vacuuming and write down the sentence that comes to mind. Then, keep going. Sometimes an image will come, sometimes a phrase. John Fowles said that the whole story of "The French Lieutenant's Woman" came from an image of a woman standing on a stone pier at the edge of the sea in England, looking back. A woman with her head turned, wearing a shawl. Everything else sprang from there. This image was the engine that fuelled the book.

Sometimes finding your idea can take a long time. Recently, with no idea of another novel in mind, but knowing that I wanted to write one, I took several months off, went to Europe, walked three hundred kilometres across Northern Spain to Santiago de Compostela and came back doubting that I would ever write another book. About five weeks later, an idea struck me. I was in the back of a car, with some friends. No reason that I could see to be struck by an idea, except that I was in a fallow state, being driven, a guest with no particular responsibilities, in a part of the country that was new to me. A sudden sense of excited urgency told me that something was up. The next day, it rained—good—and I started making notes. Something was begun. Something would be born. It was not connected directly with my long walk on the pilgrimage route through Spain, but while doing the walk, putting one foot in front of the other, sometimes painfully, sometimes miserably, but always keeping going, I had prepared the way, if you like, for something to happen in my mind.

So, if at all possible, do something you don't usually do—a boat trip, a long walk, a visit to a new place. What you will write afterwards will not necessarily be about the trip or new place or activity; no, but it will have changed you just enough for the new idea or image or sense of urgency to come in and begin to grow.

Where do you get your ideas? People often ask me this, and I have to say, I haven't the faintest idea. They arrive. Out of my life, out of a dream, out of something someone said, out of a glimpsed place, a recovered memory. Once, I used to be afraid that I would never have another one. Once a novel was finished, that would be it. But so far, it has never been "it." I may not have an idea for months or even years at a time. But sooner or later–and these days it's sooner rather than later–one shows up. Like the butterflies in my yard, which come for the passion flower vine and the humming birds that come for the little red flowers on a bush we have, they arrive; but it helps to plant what they like, what they come for, and this I try to arrange as far as possible for the ideas, too. I do find that flying helps: at around 30,000 feet, for some reason, ideas begin appearing in my head; which makes the uncomfortable business of flying these days bearable.

The Blank Page

One of the things that frightened us all as young people was the blank page handed to us in the exam room, which we were to cover with writing in a set time, and hand in to be graded or marked. A lot of people are scared of the blank page. However, an empty computer screen is less alarming, because words that are written on it don't have to be final in any way. The technology has changed so that writing something down is far less of a commitment than it used to be, even in the days of typewriters and white-out. Some people like to begin writing on actual paper, with a pen; others do cling to their typewriters. I find that the computer has liberated me so completely that it's easier to begin writing right away on my Mac screen. I can begin, play around, save, begin again, see what it looks like, juggle various versions, and so can anyone now. I'm sure it's one of the reasons that more people are writing novels and memoirs: it's just so much less laborious than it used to be.

So, open up your screen, be brave, write a good beginning, or even a bad beginning, a beginning that goes somewhere, that opens into the story that you have in you to tell. What have you got to lose? At this stage, nobody is watching. You can hide it on your desk top, in your hard drive, on a USB, or in a notebook to be locked in a drawer. It's your secret. Go on—give it a go. Remember when you learned to swim? You probably thought you were going to drown. And you surfaced, floated, and have been swimming ever since.

Keep Going

A beginning idea can seem so tiny: how can this fuel a whole book? Be extremely patient with yourself and extremely disciplined. The first draft you write will not be wonderful, or even good. That is true of us all, no matter how many novels we may have written and published. Someone has coined that phrase, "shitty first drafts" to make it sound normal. But the first draft, however shitty, has to exist for anything to happen. So, don't judge it. Keep going through all your self-doubt, don't stop until you have reached page 40. Why page 40? Because, like the first trimester of a pregnancy, this is the point at which a novel starts to exist as a real possibility. Giving up before page 40 is fatally easy to do. You think all or some of the following: I should be writing about something else, I should go back over this and correct it, this is no good, I hate it, I'm going to have to give up, I don't know what can possibly happen next, this is not the book I want to write. And so on. The point is, this is the book that seems to want you to write it, and it is the one you are actually writing. You may continue to hate it, you may hate it so much when you have finished the first draft that you want to never see it again and certainly not allow anyone else to know you have written it. But, write it. Give it a chance. It is yours, it is what you are doing. Later, you may change it so that it becomes unrecognizable, but at least you will have it, your canvas, your framework, on which to work.

Trust the process. Begin, then, continue. It sounds easy, I know, and I also know it is not. But it's the only way that I have found that works.

Page One

Actual beginnings of books, once you come (much later) to decide upon your actual beginning sentences, are like doorways into houses. They need to open smoothly and invite the reader into a hallway that's not a clutter of boxes and old furniture, mousetraps and cobwebs. You need not to leave garbage bins outside this door, and not to park your car across its entrance. Imagine you are inviting someone – an editor perhaps – into your house. Do you really want him/her to struggle to come inside, trip over things and bump into awkward corners or get covered in dust? The entrance into a book is like this. Make it welcoming, even enticing. Make the reader—the editor—want to stay. Make him/her want to see the rest of the house. Make him/her happy to be there, at ease, comfortable, interested in what you have made. These days, in which agents and editors and yes, also readers, often don't persist beyond the first page, this is crucial. It probably always was, but publishing has become so much harder and books so much more plentiful, that everyone's attention span has been shortened.

Read the beginnings of Robert Louis' Stevenson's "Treasure Island" for instant interest; then read Thomas Hardy's opening pages of "The Return of the Native" for a slow, atmospheric build-up. Each in its very different way is unforgettable.

To Plan or Not to Plan

I am often asked if I plan my novels before I begin to write them. The answer is no; it is also that my own system is probably the most time-consuming and chaotic one you could adopt. I begin to make notes, in a separate place, a notebook or journal of the book: in this I stick down everything I think of about the book. But the novel itself, I find, needs a free hand. I consult my notes and re-work them rather as you would use a road-map on a journey: the map is useful, if you want to get from A to B, but if you want to explore on the way there, you need to give yourself permission to take small side roads and stop to have a picnic, look at the view.

Many writers do make charts, lists, plans, wall-charts, all sorts of systems except a GPS. The late Iris Murdoch, for instance, plotted her books minutely, then wrote them in longhand in exercise books and gave them to someone else to type. There are many, many ways to approach a novel, and ones that rely heavily on plot may well benefit from this approach. Other writers use the metaphor of the darkened room: Virginia Woolf said that she explored the darkened room with a flashlight to discover what furniture was in it. Michael Ondaatje uses a similar analogy. I'm a darkened-room writer too, but it can and does lead to confusion. I find the road maps, notes and signposts along the way a useful tool, too. But honestly, if I knew in advance everything that was going to happen, I don't think I could be bothered to write the book: finding out, exploring, discovering, is such a great part of the pleasure.

A writer friend says that my system, or lack of system, gives him vertigo. Now, if the method described above gives you vertigo or is just too terrifying, please don't adopt it. Make a plan. Decide which scenes must take place and what the links must be. Stick your plan on the wall. Follow it. Only change it if strictly necessary. There are many ways to skin this particular cat.

A novel does have to have a shape, a structure; it has at some point to develop coherence. How organic this turns out to be is up to the individual writer. Another friend of mine who teaches literature uses "The Great Gatsby" to demonstrate an impeccable sense of structure. Yet we still don't know exactly how Fitzgerald planned it.

Some more famous beginnings:

~ Tolstoy, *Anna Karenina*: "All happy families are the same."

~ Dickens, *A Tale Of Two Cities*: "It was the best of times, it was the worst of times."

~ Daphne du Maurier, *Rebecca*: "Last night I dreamed I was at Manderley again."

Each one is unforgettable.

The magazine, "Poets and Writers" has a section where it quotes the first lines of recently published books. I always look at it and think – would I read on? Your beginning is your hook, your irresistible invitation to all the rest. Once the rest of the novel is written, it's important to go back and decide if your opening sentences are really the absolute best you can do. The beginning sets up expectations, it's the "Once Upon A Time" that enchanted us as children, it's the writer stretching out a hand to the reader and pulling her or him in. It says either, you won't be able to resist reading this book, or it says, I really don't care if you are interested or not. Some writers when young – and I was one of them – don't care about how the reader feels. They are so busy being clever young writers; they think they can get away with obscurity, clutter or obstacles put in the way of the reader. But after forty years in this business I now believe that the writer and reader make a pact, begin a conversation, begin to dance together. The beginning of a novel is an invitation to the dance.

Exercises:

Write ideas, notes, and dreams in a journal on waking. Just jot them down anyhow. If you are in the habit of writing "morning pages," (see Julia Cameron's seminal work, *The Artist's Way*) so much the better.

Go for a short walk every day. Take no money, have no other motive – no dropping by the grocery store or to see a friend, no "power walking", no errands. Just walk, and look about you.

Or go for a swim, if you live near a beach or pool, and it's warm enough.

Read the first sentence, the first paragraph of several books and write down what you think of them. Pick two or three favorites. Why do you like them? Why do others turn you off? Write your thoughts down. Be aware of what the writer is doing, and if he/she has succeeded.

Write six beginning sentences. For a mystery, a love story, a family saga, a sci-fi story, a literary thriller, a war story. Then expand each into a first paragraph.

2. CHARACTERS

Novels are about people. When we think of novels we have loved, it is nearly always the characters we remember. Characters are the progenitors of plot: we remember with affection the great characters of fiction. So, how do you get your characters?

Ways to Make Up Characters

There are several ways, and most novelists use a mixture of these. You can – and many first novels do – draw entirely from your own life and simply change the names to protect yourself from the wrath of your family. We all have several characters residing inside ourselves: the baby, the child, the teenager, the alter ego, the person we will be when old, just to name a few. You can conjure up amalgams of people you have known, or even seen in passing. You can use characters from history, safely dead, and write a historical novel. You can push it all into the future and write a sci-fi novel. Or mix all of the above. But the characters we remember are the ones who have some complexity about them, who do not stay still on the page.

Recently in my gym class we were all discussing Anna Karenina, her character and that of Vronsky. Every time I come back to that book, these people seem to have changed. It's as if they have a life inside the book that goes on when I am not looking. Other people said the same. Tolstoy was wonderful at this. Levin, in the same book, is somebody you feel you have lived with, so is his brother-in-law, Oblonsky. Jane Austen makes me feel this way about Emma, in the eponymous novel. Emma, who is infuriating, needs Mr. Knightley to put her straight about life. (Austen loses it for me in "Mansfield Park" where the characters seem to become mouthpieces for the author's ideas. What happened?) Jane Eyre is another one: we live with her, see what she has to deal with, root for her all the way, while simultaneously noticing that she is capable of snobbery, coldness and simply being wrong. Dickens' characters are rather different, in that he gives them, especially his minor characters, mannerisms and tics that identify them immediately, so that they remain the same throughout the stories.

These are some of the great 19th century novelists. What of the present? I think of the people in Toni Morrison's earlier books – "The Bluest Eye" for example. I think of Fowles' heroine in "The French Lieutenant's Woman." I think of the girl and the concierge in Muriel Barbery's "The Elegance Of The Hedgehog."

You can make your own list. Why is it harder to find memorable characters in the novels of today? Is it that we have all become more alike? That movie characters, as interpreted by actors, have taken over from the people in novels? Hana, for instance, in "The English Patient;" has she become indistinguishable from Juliette Binoche? Are we writing closer to memoir, away from sheer invention? Are we too worried that readers will not like our characters?

Letting Them Speak

Whatever is happening out there let your characters have their voice and their head. When you hear someone speaking to you as you write, get that voice down. Get the look of the person, the mannerisms, their idiosyncrasies. A novelist is like a detective in many ways: we notice people, we eavesdrop in restaurants and on buses, we speculate – what if that man coming to meet her is a lover about to deliver an ultimatum? What if they are about to break up? What if she's plotting to kill him? Read Chekhov, if you want to study character. Read "The Lady With The Little Dog." Chekhov was a doctor, which may have helped him to pay attention; close and loving attention is what you find in his stories.

Do We Have to Like Them?

There's a strange phenomenon around these days with regard to character. As the reader, you are supposed not just to empathize with a character, but to approve of her or him. This creeps even into reviews and criticism. It may go some way to explaining why characters in novels seem to have become blander. They are not supposed to be selfish, limited, or, God forbid, immoral. Think of Dostoevsky when you come across this trend: think of Raskolnikov, or the Brothers Karamazov. Think also of Camus' main character in "The Stranger." Toni Morrison achieves, in her fiction, the feat of showing how limited or even cruel a person can be and yet allowing us to understand him or her. This is a triumph of novelistic imagining. Far too many characters in fiction these days appear flat, simply because we are supposed to like them and empathize with them all the time.

Spend time thinking about your characters. It beats worrying about your own family or friends. You can make your characters in your novel do what you want, for a start. Spend time imagining them. What would they do, say, change if you let them go their own way? I used to think it rather whimsical and fey when writers said that their characters ran away with them, disobeyed them, insisted on having things their own way. Then I began to experience it more and more, as I improvised dialogue between them, let them dream and fantasize, even let characters appear in stories where their presence had not been invited. Fanciful? Try it sometime. Begin some dialogue, let them talk.

Making Them Move

Start a scene in which you aren't sure of the outcome. Do it for fun, for experience, and then see. You may not want to incorporate it in your final version, but it will at least allow you to know the characters better. If all they ever do and all you know about them appears between the covers of your book, they will not give the sense of having a life outside the book. They will appear too willed. So, write about them in your notebook, ask them questions, find out what they want. Most of the action in novels springs from the desire of people to have what can't easily be had. Ask yourself, what do my characters want? Then, what do they want next? Desire – and I don't mean simply sexual desire – is the fuel of most novels. They are about human wanting, more than anything else.

Changing the Names!

Novelists sometimes get into trouble because real life friends or acquaintances, and above all, families, see themselves in the characters. Well, of course, nobody can make up a character from scratch. Our families are our first environment, they are where we learn to notice and be fascinated by human behavior (and to suffer from it). In this situation, my advice is, simply lie. Change the names and brave it out. A novelist friend of mine gave me this advice twenty-five years ago. Say, I made it up. Take the line of least resistance. "No, see, she really isn't you, she has red hair and a Pomeranian, not black hair and a Lab." Some people like "finding themselves" in novels; others simply hate it. A relative of mine reminds me so often that I am not to "put her in a novel" that I have to mention it here; and simultaneously say, this is impossible, nobody can put somebody else in a novel, because my perception is only my perception, and I don't have the power – nobody does – to write a real person's complexity into a character in a book.

Novelists lie. We lie in order to tell the truth.

Character as Fate

Character is fate, in a novel. Our fictional characters may change and have insights, but as their creators we need to have them being more or less consistent. That is to say, their ability to change has to be earned in the course of the novel. (See again, "Emma.")   Arbitrary change will alienate the reader. Gradual, earned change will fascinate him/her.

Minor characters need to be as interesting, in their way, as major ones. You may have one main character, or two, or six. But, they will be surrounded by others, who deserve as much attention, even if they only get a paragraph or two on the page, as the main people.   Understudies, people with bit parts, have to rehearse just as much as the main actors, in a stage play, and the same is true of a novel. Don't have anyone whose job is transparently to move the action on, or to explain a point. Make these minor characters real too. This is a work of imagination, and imagination has to be allowed full play in a novel.

Don't let your plot is get in the way of your characters. The plot depends on them, not the other way around. And even if you have a brilliant, original plot idea, if you let it run the show, you will end up being boring – or at least, only having your book read once, on an airplane, and left behind on the seat once the journey is over. Readers will read almost anything in the air, to keep their minds off the idea of instant death; once they come down to earth, they don't want your plot-driven blockbuster any more and will gladly leave it behind rather than carry it home. I've seen this happen, over and over.

You want your book to be at someone's bedside, for months or years on end; to be the one they don't want to lend out, in case it disappears; to be the one read and re-read, appreciated for its insights over and over. I have one of these books at my bedside, and it's Michael Ondaatje's "In the Skin of a Lion." I defy anyone to leave that on a plane.

Welcoming the Reader In

How many characters should you have? As many as you can comfortably fit in your mind and care about. That is, not too many. A cast of hundreds is confusing. In the 19th century, when the great Russian novels began to appear, they would often be published – and still are – with a list of characters at the beginning, name, patronymic, surname. Sometimes there were family trees.

But at this point, beware of introducing too many characters at the very beginning, because the reader will get scared off, or at least confused. We want just one or two people to welcome us into the house. More may appear later, but it's very hard, even in life, to be introduced to a whole bunch of people in a few minutes, and most of us can't focus enough to remember names, let alone anything else.

Let the reader in gently. Let him/her get a look at

these characters, come up close to them, shake their hands, have time to notice what is interesting about them. Make your reader want to get to know them more thoroughly, want to hear their stories, get some clue about what they are going to do.

Beware of having one character meander about being introspective. A novel is about social inter-action, about meeting and things happening from that meeting, it is about human beings coming together, doing something, drawing you in to what they are doing. Some experimental novels – the Nouveau Roman in France, for example – tried to change all that, and simply gave you an empty room to wander about it on your own. I'm not saying that isn't interesting, rather as Nouvelle Cuisine was interesting, challenging some preconceptions about what dinner was. But, if you are not Robbe-Grillet, and you are not, don't try it. Or, don't try it until you are sixty and have published several successful traditional novels. Don't risk it as a first try.

Making Them Live

When I was young – I mean, really young, ten or eleven or twelve - I would start out with my characters, describe each of them minutely, down to what they were wearing; their hair, skin, eye color, what they liked, what they disliked. They were nearly always members of a big family: the more, the merrier. I set them out like those paper dolls you can dress, with their peculiarities, their unique and fascinating selves. But I could never think what to do with them. They stood there, waiting for a story, waiting for the action. They were what E.M. Forster in his "Aspects of the Novel" called "flat" characters. I could not make them move. I loved doing this, but knew that there had to be more. How do you move your characters about? How do you animate them? How do you make them live? My solution was to have another, different, family move in next door and describe them, in minute detail. But, the same sticking point occurred. I had two families of characters, but still they would not move. I had no authorial voice; so they just stood there, on the page, staring back at me. Time after time, I got my characters lined up, then abandoned the whole idea. What was it that needed to happen?

They needed to be given a shove and made to move. Start talking to each other, start arguing, start being attracted to each other, start being jealous, angry, in love, competitive, whatever human beings can be. Start wanting things. Start living.

POV

This, Point of View as it is called, is about who gets to tell the story, or through whose eyes we see it.

You can have one person telling it, or alternate chapter to chapter, or abandon the whole human enterprise and have a tiger on a life-raft, as in "The Life of Pi" or a green lady lizard, as in Michael Cunningham's bewitching "Specimen Days."

It's up to you; but a word of warning: it gets complicated. Switching POV too often can confuse the reader, and you. Try to be sure whose story this is, before you get too far in, and stick to that person through thick and thin. Many, many novels have had an "omniscient" narrator – one who like God can see into everyone's minds and tell you about them. This is the way of the 19th-century novel. Many have had a first person – the "I" – through whose eyes and brain or stream of consciousness we interpret the whole novel. "Treasure Island", "Jane Eyre", "Moby Dick." Many have been successful in switching between two or even three characters' points of view. But once you have decided which you want to do, hang in there as far as possible. Also, decide on a first person or third person narration.

Whose story is this? Ask yourself early on, and identify the main protagonist, or hero/heroine.

Exercises:

Go to a café, bar or restaurant, observe someone or a couple of people, imagine who they might be, where they are from, what their relationship might be. If you are close enough, write down some of what they are saying. When you get home, write some imaginary dialogue between them, using what you noticed.

Follow an (adult) person in the street for twenty minutes, notice every detail you can about them: clothes, way of walking, anything odd, interesting. Yes, being a writer is sometimes like being a detective, or spy.

Make a list of eccentric people you have known and what made them interesting.

Write a description of a character based on the one you followed in the street, or on an eccentric relative.

If anyone challenges you while doing any of

the above, say you are doing research for a novel, or casting for a movie. They will generally be delighted that you chose them. They probably won't call the police.

3. PLOT

What is It?

A confession, another one. For many years, I had simply no idea what people were talking about when they mentioned Plot. The Gunpowder Plot, yes. Plot in the novel, no. The reason was that I grew up reading the Modernists, Woolf, Joyce, Calvino, and was convinced that this was now what the novel had to be. It was impossible to do, of course, but you had to try. Later, I went back to these writers – Woolf, par excellence – and realized that she is extremely good at plot, you just don't notice her doing it. The plot, for instance, of Mrs. Dalloway is extremely clear, it all takes place during one day, Septimus has shell-shock, or Post-Traumatic Stress Syndrome after the first World War, Mrs. D. has her party, the two lives beautifully intertwine and meet when he falls on her railings and kills himself. And, in "To The Lighthouse," the plot is exemplary: pre-war, war, post-war; characters come together, part, come back together again; the plan to go to the Lighthouse begins the book, and is accomplished at its end.

Neat, really.

When people lectured me on Plot, I imagined it like something out of Sherlock Holmes, with clues, traps and a denouement (aha!) and I didn't think I could do that. So I pretended plot did not matter, and my first novels, mercifully unpublished, were ones in which people had insights (aha!) but nothing much happened. I got hooked on Marguerite Duras, who can make someone having a phone call in an empty house quite fascinating. I felt, for a long time, lost at sea.

What Happens?

Plot is, I now think, simply a word for What Happens. For something does have to happen in a novel, for people to want to read it. The reader has to want to take part in the book – be in on the plot, care about what happens – sufficiently for him or her to take time out of their own fascinating lives to enter our novels. It is no good just lining up your characters and hoping for the best.

So, how do you know What Happens? How do you convey what a writer friend of mine calls "The Aboutness?" It takes time. What the book ends up being about, is not always or even often what it started out being about. It takes time, and at some point you will need to put on your critic's hat, or better, find a good reader, in order to find out what you have done.

Have you told a story? Because, after all is

said and done, that is what a novel is. It's linear, it's narrative, it has stuff happening. Back in the 1960's I never thought I'd say that. But in 2010, it is what I have learned is true.

But

What happens does not have to be full of twists and turns, or have a surprise ending. The old idea that a reader needs to be surprised has really gone out of the window. What I think a reader is looking for is intelligence on the page. We want, as readers, to be entertained, yes, but also to understand something. The narrative that is the novel must take us to a place we have not been to before. We want to be in the company of someone intelligent as we go there, to be able to trust the writer. Not necessarily trust the narrator – think of "The Great Gatsby" in which it is not Nick who has an accurate perception of Gatsby, but Fitzgerald. Think of "The Remains Of The Day" by Kazuo Ishiguro, who is notoriously good at this.

This desire to meet another human intelligence has been with us since birth. We come into this world hoping to meet another intelligence: sometimes it happens, sometimes not. We often go to school for the first time, hoping the same thing, and are so often disappointed. We fall in love, because we see the gleam of something special in someone else. And we read, in order to find that intelligence on the page: to trust that we will be taken somewhere, and not disappointed once again.

So, as writers, we have to deploy our intelligence. Writing a novel is not just about expressing our unique view of the world: it is about developing the ability to make someone else want to see it too. To come along. To play. To join in the adventure. Are we up to it?

Recycling

All plots have been used before. There are the classics: someone comes to town, someone leaves town and goes somewhere new. Many of the Jane

Austen plots are the former: new rich handsome young man shows up in the neighborhood, everyone wants to meet him. Charlotte Bronte's "Jane Eyre," conversely, is about someone who goes somewhere new, because she has to get a job, she can't just sit there in the neighborhood and wait. Maybe the difference between these plots is about class.

Other much-used plots:

~ Someone falls in love with someone they are not supposed to, so the plot is about forbidden, or crossed, love. "The Great Gatsby" and a thousand others.

~ Someone kills someone. Who, why and what is the outcome? The plot of thrillers and detective novels.

~ Someone travels to a new place and learns things about the place and him/herself; this is the "Eat, Pray, Love" formula in novel form.

~ Someone wants to go to a new place but doesn't make it: "Revolutionary Road."

~ Someone goes to a magical place and can't find it again: "Le Grand Meaulnes." ("The Lost Domain")

~ A whole set of people live through a time in history, their own, and learn things about themselves and it: the novels of Jonathan Franzen, Colm Toibin, Calum McCann's "Let the Great World Spin".

~ The world is ending: what happens to the few people left in it? The recent novels of Margaret Atwood and Cormac MacCarthy.

Sometimes we get something extraordinary, that nobody else has thought of: that tiger on the life raft, "The Life of Pi." But the shipwreck story, the rescue story, the days and nights at sea, all this has been done before.

So your story will not be new. But it will be new to you, and therefore new (we hope) to your readers. Don't strain for originality: let originality come. Tell your story patiently, hopefully, determinedly. It has all been done before; and none of it has been done before. You are in the company of thousands of other writers; and, you are dizzyingly, thrillingly alone.

Theme

What is the difference, if any, between Plot and Theme?

Plot is what actually takes place, leading us from A to B to C. Theme is what we want readers to understand about it. Theme is not stated, in most novels. Writers want intelligent readers to work it out on their own. Theme is the novel's relation to the era in which it is written, to other novels; to the reader's own life, to the zeitgeist. Franzen's novel "The Corrections" was about a group of people in a family, its plot was contained in their relationships, its theme was that a correction must take place in society; its success was that others picked up and understood this theme, and that a great big "correction" actually happened out there in the world.

Plot is what happens on the ground, theme is what happens in the air. Plot is dynamic, theme ethereal. Many reviewers, mistakenly, tell the plot of a novel without commenting on its theme. Good reviewers start with the theme and its connection to the rest of life. Theme is connected to "Aboutness." When somebody asks what your novel is about, they don't really want to be told the plot, but something in them is sniffing after the theme, and wondering, will it connect with anything in my life, will it take me somewhere, will it move me on? Theme is what, as a writer, you sometimes suddenly discover after writing a first draft. "Oh, is that what I've been writing about?"

AHA!

The revelation of what the theme is can arrive quite late in the day. When I was younger, working on a typewriter, I used to have to write out the whole of each of my novels in order to discover what it was about. Then I would start again. Oh, so *that*'s what it's all about! Typing, every single word, in the light of what I had only just discovered. Time-wasting, perhaps: yet somehow, essential. I think if I had not labored so over those early drafts, I would not be in the slightly more aware place that I am now.

Rewrite!

Rewriting is an essential part of writing; I can't emphasize this strongly enough.

Rewriting, you get a chance to dig out the theme, elaborate it, make it more evident. It's like archeology: if you haven't labored to dig up all those individual bones and shards, you can't even hazard a guess at what the site was for and who lived there, and when.

Narrative Drive

This is another aspect of plot and theme. Editors used to write me kind rejection letters pointing out that my novels lacked narrative drive. I didn't know what they meant, and it drove me nuts. I was busy doing interesting juxtapositions, flashbacks, dreams, jumps into the future, alternative points of view. I was hooked on the gymnastics of the modern novel. Then, working with kind and patient editors, I began to learn. Narrative drive is the fuel that drives the whole engine of the novel forward; and a novel that hasn't any is a train sitting in a siding. Interesting to look at, perhaps; but going nowhere.

You have to use your voice – or the narrator's, or the characters' – to drive your novel on. You know it when you see it; you feel it when you have done it. But do not blame yourself for having difficulty with it; it is one of the hardest aspects of novel writing. It is also one of the essentials, because it is what captures and keeps the reader's attention. For some reason, we are more tolerant of movies that are all over the place, that play with connections that are so loose we don't get them. Perhaps it is because it's an effort to get up and leave the movie theatre. But in a novel, if there is no sense of design, no narrative drive, we get discouraged. Why are we reading this, if the writer is taking us nowhere? So we put it down.

Narrative drive is very close to story, or plot. That sense of the falling of dominoes one after the other, at once effortless and necessary, but never forced, is what makes a story work.

Causality

The wheel of cause and effect, X leading to Y and on to Z – or not – is another way of imagining it. Simply having things happen is not enough. To be able to connect your events, to create a smooth flow, even using different narratives or different points of view, is a skill that takes a lot of work to achieve. Too tight a linkage of cause and effect and you lose your reader; too loose and you risk the same thing. Beware of randomness. Life is more random then fiction can dare to be, as it is also more full of coincidences than fiction can risk – modern fiction, anyway. If you love coincidence, go to the great 19th-century Russian novelists, or Hardy, or Dickens. But be wary of using it too freely in a contemporary novel because you'll strain the reader's belief, and you want that belief on your side.

Rule–Breaking

One of my favorite stories is in a collection by John Fowles, "The Ebony Tower," in which a detective sets out to solve a crime and then simply ignores the crime as he begins falling in love. But to be able to subvert or ignore cause and effect, or play with genre, you have to be very familiar with what you are subverting or ignoring. It's like cooking: only when you are familiar with a recipe can you begin to cook without it and make the dish your own way.

Exercises:

Write down, fast, the most absurd plot line or story that you can.

Get together with a friend and spend a day making up a novel. I once did this on a rainy day in Scotland with a fellow writer and we had huge fun and came up with a dramatic plot that in fact we never used. It's so much easier doing this with another person.

What are your three favorite novels? What, if anything, do they have in common? Where does this common theme touch your own life? Journal on this.

Do the same with your three favorite movies. Any noticeable shared themes? Any connection with your own life/dream/memories? What are your beloved topics, the ones that really fascinate you?

What is the one story in your life that is uniquely yours? The one nobody else could possibly tell?

4. GETTING UNSTUCK

Getting unstuck assumes that you have got stuck in the first place. It's safe to assume this: there will be a place where your novel seems to have become stuck. Don't worry, as this always happens at some point. You are far from being alone.

Jump Starts

Here are some ways of jump-starting a stalled story. You have already walked round the block, wailed at your nearest and dearest, contemplated a drink or a large sweet something to eat, decided that it's hopeless and that you must begin again.

Go back and face the story and begin reading it, underlining or marking the parts that are simply non-negotiable, because you like them so much. I know, a lot has been written and said about "murdering your darlings" but this is not the time and place for that. Cherish your darlings. Notice just how good the good bits are. Reread them and find out what they are telling you: they are the foundations from which you will move on.

Then begin, gently, slowly, to write more in that vein, even if it doesn't seem to fit. Sometimes novels have been too strictly planned in advance, so that there is no room for inspiration. Improvise. Play around a bit. Take one character and write more about him/her. The only reason you got stuck was that you could not yet imagine how to continue, and this is so normal to all writers that it is never worth worrying about.

If the stuckness persists, put your novel in a

drawer, or somehow refuse to look at it on your computer for a week or two, or more. Then, when you get it out again, something will have happened. You will know how to move it on.

An excellent tip, from Ernest Hemingway, was to leave a paragraph or sentence unfinished when you stop work, so that you can pick it up the next day. It's like leaving yourself a trail, a mark in the forest. Finishing that unfinished sentence will mean you are writing already, and will write on. Taking the first step, writing the first few words, will move you on. Silence the harsh voice that says repeatedly, this isn't any good. Tell it you don't care. Tell it you don't care if anyone ever likes this story, because that's not why you are writing it. Follow the trail you have marked for yourself, to where it leads, and beyond. What you write will not be like anyone's else's book; but that is the whole point, whatever marketing departments like to say about books resembling each other or like horses, being bred out of Anne Rice by Jonathan Franzen, or whatever. The whole point is to write something unlike everyone else, and if you follow your own trail that is what you will do.

A simple trick that I have found very useful is to choose some theme music for your novel, a certain song, a certain piece of mood music. Every time you sit down to write, start by playing this theme song. It will get you back into the mood of the novel. By the time the music stops, if it does, you'll already be well on your way. Use just one song or piece, not a medley.

Another good way to find continuity is to write in the same place and if possible, at the same time each day, so that you go physically to meet your book and it awaits you. I find it helpful to leave the house in the morning and go to a studio a block away. At the very least, have a room where you can shut the door.

Taking the Time It Takes

Sometimes a novel will stay stalled for years. I

have had this happen, because at the time when I had the original idea, I simply could not work out the form and structure or see what needed to happen. When this happens, begin something else. Make sure you have saved your original one, and come back to it. My "Becoming George Sand" was first begun in the mid 1980's and was finally published in 2010, believe it or not. In between, I wrote several other novels. Then, one day in 2006, I took the stained, dog-eared type-written mess out of my closet and began to look at it with fresh eyes. It had needed those twenty years, for some reason, to come to fruition.

Jean Rhys spent twenty years on her last novel, "Wide Sargasso Sea." Sometimes, time needs to elapse, life has to go on, books have to be written and rewritten; who really knows why?

Practice

The important thing is to go on writing, write when you think you have nothing to say, write when you can, when you must, when you're asked to, when you're paid to and when you're not paid to. It's all about developing the right habits, the right attitude and the right eye; if you want to be good at tennis, play tennis, not once a year but all the time; if you want to play the piano, the same goes; if you want to write well, keep writing. It's not all going to be gold, some of it is sure to be dross; but you won't know the difference unless you do it and do it and do it.

Exercises:

Go for another walk, somewhere if possible you have not been before. Go to a movie, an art gallery, a concert – immerse yourself in other forms of art.

Re-read the first pages of a novel you love. This will remind you why you wanted to write a novel in the first place.

Look at what you are doing in order to stay stuck. Have you had houseguests? A major public holiday, e.g., Christmas? Have you gone out of your way to give time to someone else? All of the above are fine in themselves but do in my experience lead to feeling stuck. Anything you do which interrupts your normal routine or flow can lead to problems.

Be honest: are you drinking, eating, shopping more than usual? Have you been to a lot of parties? Who has interrupted you, if anyone? What bad old pattern crept back into your life? Don't blame yourself, but be honest. We all fall off the horse and have to pick ourselves up and get back on.

Promise yourself a treat when you have finished your first draft: a trip, a vacation, a party, a spa, a period of lying in a hammock doing nothing.

Then go back to the novel and start writing, write for an hour without stopping, and then stop. Congratulate yourself: you have come unstuck.

5. ENDINGS

A novel has to end, just as a life does. But THE END in a novel signifies something quite other than the end of life. Something has to have happened, usually, that makes sense of all the rest. Something has to pull together the narrative, not just abandon it.

Famous Endings

Some famous endings are very different from one another. Tolstoy, at the end of "War and Peace" ties up all his loose ends, like a good historian. Natasha marries Pierre, and they have children, and life goes on. We are told almost more than we want to know. Another famous one is the modernist Henry Green's ending: "The next day they went on very much as before." Which, in its way, echoes Tolstoy's. Novelists have given us shock endings, denouement endings, baffling endings, double endings ("The French Lieutenant's Woman"), trick endings, happily-ever-after endings, endings where you turn the page and feel as if you'd fallen off a cliff, because suddenly there is no more. I personally appreciate an ending which connects both with what has gone before and with what comes after: that makes a statement about the past of the novel, everything I have read so far, but also reaches out into the immediate future, so that there's a sense of promise rather than a cliff-edge. It's a tall order, I know.

Don't Worry

Don't worry about the ending, but bear it in mind. Some people write their endings first and work towards them through the whole book, rather as Woody Allen in "Play It Again, Sam" works towards a situation in which his hero can speak, in context, the words which Humphrey Bogart speaks at the end of "Casablanca."

Sometimes an ending will just occur to you, as you write. Sometimes it will be an image that expresses completion, as in "To The Lighthouse" when Lily has had her vision. Sometimes, if you are very lucky, you will suddenly glimpse the ending as you work towards it, and it falls into your novel as a ripe apple falls from the tree. Other times, you will have to toil and toil to get it. People are fond of "epiphanies" in fiction, or moments when the character suddenly realizes something. In "coming of age" novels, these moments signify the growth to maturity of the protagonist.

PLAY AROUND with endings. Try this and then that. Allow time. Ask yourself: what is it that I want to say before I end this book, and have I said it? Ask yourself, what would happen if I ended it *here?*

Sometimes a story or novel goes "past it's ending." The writer has wanted to make sure that you, the reader, has really got it, what he/she was trying to say. You can tell, if you are the writer, when you have gone past your true ending: your listener or reader starts to display signs of impatience or restlessness.

Don't talk down to your reader. Assume that where you originally wanted to end the book is just fine, and no more explanation is needed. Try it both ways, then one way again, then the other. How do you really want to end your book? It's like ending a meal: do you want the reader to feel satisfied, ready for a little coffee, wanting to go on sipping her wine, digesting what she has already swallowed, enjoying the pause after eating; or do you want her to dash up and out immediately and on to the next thing – the next book in her pile of things to read, to get through – forgetting yours almost immediately? Do you want that succulent last mouthful you gave her to linger in her taste buds for hours, even days? Think about it. What will make any reader go back to the beginning and begin to reread? Most novelists would give anything for this to happen.

We want to be flies on the wall when a reader arrives at the end of our book, smiles and goes right back to the beginning. As Nabokov said, we all write to be reread. So, you have to have given your reader something that is worth rereading: and that means, some intelligence, some grace in the writing, a view of the world which cannot easily be put down, a sense of delight which is worth holding on to.

Revision

I can't say this strongly enough: revision is at the heart of good writing. If you don't want to revise, don't even begin! Revision is what makes the reader want to reread, it gives the book its final form, it weeds out the unnecessary, it emphasizes what matters, it links the parts, it is what makes the coherent whole of a novel. Revise, revise, revise. Revise as a sculptor polishes marble, chisels wood. Go on until you are sick of it, and then go on some more. Learn to enjoy it as an integral part of writing. Oh, good, now I get to revise again! This should be the response to any rejection or criticism. Revision strengthens the container that is your book, making it watertight and elegant.

Exercises:

Visit a cemetery and read the statements on tombstones. No, this is not to give you an ending for your novel or give you a taste for the morbid, or even to remind you how short your life may be. It just makes you aware of how life does end, and of how people interpret it. Then be glad you are still alive! Write your own gravestone comment: here lies Jane Smith, writer. Or whatever. Make up a great epitaph for yourself. (E.g., Wilfred Sheed: "He wrote some good sentences.")

Write some absurd last paragraphs, just for fun. This exercise is to allow you to lighten up around endings.

When I was young, a cousin used to tell us stories in which you knew the ending was approaching when a pewter plate appeared in the narrative. The ending was always the same: "The pewter plate bended, and my story's ended." What other devices can you use for hinting that the narrative is coming to an end? Write a couple of short last chapters, using these devices.

What sort of ending do you like? Puzzling, revelatory, an epiphany, or "happy ever after"? Why do you think this is?

6. STYLE

The topic of style is a complex one. Or very simple, depending on which way you look at it. Another paradox. Your style is your trademark; it is as personal as the way you walk; and not many people copy the way others walk – or at least not without looking ridiculous. Style is the way you say things. It's the way you choose words, put sentences together, create paragraphs. It's the coherence of your novel, its face on the page. It's about rhythm, movement, breath.

Clarity

As a beginning novelist, try to write as clearly as possible. Use nouns and verbs: only necessary adjectives, as few adverbs as possible. Put pronouns, prepositions in the right place, use straightforward grammar. Build up from sentences to paragraphs. Check for repetitions, non-sequiturs, long-windedness, tautology. Have you said what you mean? Are you conscious of what you mean to say?

Use short words where possible, words based in Anglo-Saxon, rather than Latinate ones. Of course, long words such as "alligator" or "encephalitis" are fine, as they are the only ones that express the reality of that animal, that disease. But beware of using a Latinate word where an Anglo-Saxon one will do. E.g. don't use "commence", use "begin." Don't write "beverage" when you mean, "drink." Keep it simple, keep it simple, keep it simple.

Try to use the active rather than the passive

voice. Check each sentence for unnecessary baggage. All of us have a tendency to repeat ourselves without realizing it.

There is a peculiar notion around that good writing is flowery writing. Far too many inexperienced writers indulge in what is called "purple prose" – e.g., flowery, verbose writing for the sake of sounding impressive. So, when you check your sentences and paragraphs, make sure that it's there for a good reason. Alternating plain prose and something more fancy can make a novel more enjoyable because more nuanced – you don't have to do the same thing all the time.

Good Design

Good style is unobtrusive, elegant because functional, satisfying because it tells you just enough of what you need to know. It doesn't trip up the reader. It's like good design. In a well-designed house you don't always have to be gasping in admiration, you just feel comfortable, at ease, and you don't worry about bumping into things, falling down steps, or coming face to face with an ornate decoration that has no apparent use. Read your prose aloud to hear how it sounds, and if it trips you up, it will certainly trip the reader. It should sound fluent, easy, even if writing it is has been long and hard.

Drafts

Your first draft, your second draft, your third draft will not show any signs of style. First draft is jamming things down, roughing out a story. Second draft is finding out what you have written and cleaning it up. Third draft is beginning to look at how you have used the language. Only Noel Coward was sure enough of himself to say he'd written a play in four days. Most novelists or at least the ones who earn our respect, have written their books over and over again.

Study Others' Style

Style, of course, has its historical roots. Read Melville, Mark Twain, Henry James, Nabokov, all great stylists from different periods of history. Compare Jane Austen and Charlotte and Emily Bronte with any contemporary English woman writer. Hear the different cadences of English and American speech, as well as the pitch and swell of how language has been used at different times, in different places. All this is the education of a writer, and will tell you how to find and follow your own style. As I said at the beginning of this book, we learn by imitation. Yet we progress by daring. Trying and testing, reading and rereading, cutting and pruning, all this is part of the whole long enterprise that is your novel.

Exercises:

Try cutting every other sentence in any paragraph and see what you are left with. (You can always put some of it back). So often, less is more.

Read aloud, first to yourself, then to somebody else. See which parts make you uncomfortable? See which words, sentences, paragraphs you would like to omit?

Apart from the wide reading suggested above, read isolated paragraphs of well-known novels and see what you think works and what doesn't. The critics are not always right. This way, you can develop your own critical eye.

Put your manuscript away for at least three months, then get it out, read it through, underline everything that you don't think is necessary, on this fresh reading with your newly fresh eye.

7. YOUR READER

Who?

I have written from time to time here about "your reader." Who is this person? When you are writing your novel you don't want to be thinking of him/her at all, nor trying to second-guess reactions. When you are writing, there is just you and the novel. But you hope, posit, trust at the same time that there will be a person like the one addressed by Charlotte Bronte when she wrote, "Reader, I married him."

Your novel is addressed to this imaginary Reader,

but you don't want to be conscious of him/her? Yes, that's just about it; that's the paradox of writing fiction. It's for you, and not for you. It's private, intensely personal, and designed to go public. It starts inside and moves outside. Like all art, it belongs to you alone and to the world.

But there is also in another sense "a reader": the person you ask to read your manuscript before sending it out into the world. This is no imaginary person reading alone in a restaurant, on a plane, on a Kindle, in the bath, in bed. This is someone you know and trust.

This reader is a person to be treasured, honored, respected. Someone is taking time out of his/her life to read your book. Be nice to him or her. Be very, very grateful.

Let's Jump Ahead

Let's imagine that you have written your novel to your own – occasional – satisfaction: how do you know if you will interest a reader, even slightly? The imaginary Reader, that is, the one you have tried not to think about, the one reading alone far from where you are. You don't. This is outside your control. But you can choose a helpful person to be your first reader in a practical sense.

Most of us veer from imagining ourselves winning a Pulitzer to hiding our heads in total shame after interesting nobody at all. Reality always exists somewhere between extremes. No writer is perfect, no book is perfect; nobody deserves to be shamed, few books, unless they are totally obscene or totally propagandist, are completely unreadable. So, try to put the extremes to one side and think who do I want as my first reader? Pick somebody you trust, another writer – he or she will know what you are struggling with – and set up an exchange. The help and criticism you receive will exactly equal the help and criticism you give. If this turns out not to be so, pick some one else. Or find a reputed editor, and pay him or her. Do not give your novel to your lover, your spouse, your parents, your best friend: not because they don't have their interests at heart, but because the advice or comment you get will not be purely professional.

To My Beloved...

I know that some people dedicate their novels to "my wife, without whose dedicated reading I would never have..." Or "my husband, my perfect first reader." It may work, for them. It worked for Virginia Woolf, who handed her finished manuscripts to her husband Leonard and suffered agonies while he took off to the summerhouse to read them. He would come out each time, saying "Your best yet. A work of genius." Well, it happened that he was a writer and a publisher, and he was also broadly speaking right. But he was also a husband trying to prevent his wife from having another nervous breakdown. He could have been jealous of her success, privately bored, he could have felt that it was not really "her best yet." All I'm saying here is that in a relationship there are usually too many other things going on for the critic to feel free to comment.

SET UP a reliable relationship with another writer who knows what you are trying to do, who appreciates and loves your work, who isn't afraid to make comments and criticize. This person is worth cherishing.

If you are on a desert island, read aloud to the birds. Then at least you will be able to hear what is right and what is wrong with your prose. Reading aloud is a real test. Unfortunately, some writers wait till they are reading their published work at a public reading before they read it aloud. The shock of reading your own verbose sentences can make you want to rewrite when it's already way too late to do so. So, find someone to read to, read it aloud to yourself, or the cat, or the potted palm if there isn't a human around, but read it aloud: simply to save yourself embarrassment and pain at some future date when you are asked to read at some literary event, do it now. Then cross out or erase all the bits you didn't enjoy reading.

SO, you have a manuscript, someone else beside yourself has read it, or heard it, and likes it. What now?

Put it Away

Put it away again, for at least six months, was the advice given to me by Annie Dillard; you will not find a better writer and reader than she in this world.

Then look at it again. It will be like coming back into your house after a long journey: you will see immediately what doesn't work, what needs painting, what needs to be fixed, what you could change. Because *you* will have changed. Whether you will do the fixing is another matter; it's so easy to slip back into the thing you recognize, comfy as an old shoe.

My daughter, on returning from Australia when she was eighteen, walked back into the house and said, "You still have that half-empty pot of marmalade exactly where it was when I left." But it took me leaving, my own journey to Australia, if you like, to see what she meant and move far more than the pot of marmalade.

The dusty pot of marmalade that's still there in your novel may have to go. Or not. But at least you will get to think about whether it should still be there on that shelf.

WHEN six months are up and you look at your novel again, get to work. Cut, paste, add, above all cut. Computers can cut swathes through a book in no time at all, so keep your early drafts, but don't look at them again. Look at this new, shorn thing you have, so much better for its slimming regime and its haircut. It is most likely getting closer to something that an agent might actually want to read.

NEVER send anything to an agent or publisher that you are at all unsure about. It's so tempting to fire it off right away: pressing SEND is so much easier than printing out, doing up a package, trekking to the Post Office and buying stamps. For a visual version of how it used to be, see Jane Campion's movie "My Brilliant Life." In most current movies, writers are always shown getting immediate responses on cell phones from love-struck agents/ publishers and excitedly opening bottles of champagne. Very rarely, except in Woody Allen movies, does any novel get turned down. But in life it happens all the time. Prepare yourself for disappointment – if this is a thing that's possible to do. Remind yourself: I will get dozens, scores, even hundreds of rejections. Being rejected is what a writer's life is about. If this sounds masochistic, then remind yourself that each rejection letter is a sign that you are serious about this. Luckily, for people who can't bear to go through all this anguish, there are other routes to publication these days: publishing on-line, self-publishing, small press co-publishing, print-on-demand. The Internet is full of details about the above, and very many good books are now published by these alternative methods.

IF you are determined to go the traditional route and have an established publishing house buy your book and pay you royalties, then remember these things:

Never Forget

The publishing industry is in turmoil at present as it deals with electronic publishing, the demise of bookstores, all the changes in print literature that are appearing – e.g., Kindle – and the shrinking market for literary fiction. The whole economy is making publishers buy fewer books.

Your book is one of thousands being sent out at the same time.

You will receive rejections. Lots of them, some of

them polite, regretful; others, curt.

You will be a writer if you keep on writing anyway.

You will be a writer if you adopt one of the alternative ways of publishing listed above.

You will only stop being a writer if you stop writing, which means working at it, as hard and as well as you can, pushing yourself always to write at the top of your form.

Somebody still has to be published, and it might as well be you.

...

A Final Word

Whenever anything good or positive happens to you in your writing career, celebrate! Open that bottle of champagne. A writer at a writers' convention once recommended this, reminding us all that we are dealing with hard realities and many disappointments on a regular basis. So, when the story gets accepted, the poem published, the novel comes out, celebrate! Raise a glass, even if its ginger ale, throw a party and tell people why.

THEN – well, you already know what I'm going to say next: get back to work!

PS: It's really only worthwhile doing all of the above if you can't bear the idea of not writing. Enjoy it! Even the hard bits. And, great good luck go with you.

THE END FOR NOW

A FEW RECOMMENDED BOOKS:

"First we read; then we write" Robert D. Richardson

"How Fiction Works" James Wood, Farrar, Straus 2008

"Literature and the Taste of Knowledge"
Michael Wood, Cambridge University Press, 2005

"The Writing Life" Annie Dillard, Harper Perennial 1990

"A Reader's Manifesto" B.R. Myers, Melville House 2002

"The Artist's Way" Julia Cameron, Putnam 1992

"On Writing: A Memoir of the Craft" Stephen King

ABOUT THE AUTHOR:

Rosalind Brackenbury is an English writer living in Key West, Florida. She has published twelve novels, five collections of poetry and prize-winning short stories. She has moderated at the Key West Literary Seminar and was Writer in Residence at the College of William and Mary, Williamsburg VA in 2006; she teaches free-lance workshops as well as classes at the Studios of Key West and is a co-founder of the Key West Writers' Lab, set up in 2011 to provide coaching and mentorship for writers. Learn more at www.KeyWestWritersLab.org.

www.ingramcontent.com/pod-product-compliance
Lightning Source LLC
LaVergne TN
LVHW091314080426
835510LV00007B/490